When To Say Yes!

And Make More Friends

Sharon Scott

HUMAN RESOURCE
DEVELOPMENT PRESS

Amherst, Massachusetts

Copyright © 1988 by
Human Resource Development Press, Inc.
22 Amherst Road, Amherst, Massachusetts 01002
(413) 253-3488 (Mass.)
1-800-822-2801 (outside Mass.)

All rights reserved. Printed in the United States of America. No part of the material protected by this copyright notice may be reproduced or utilized in any form or by any means, electronic or mechanical, including photocopying, recording, or by information storage and retrieval system without written permission from the copyright owner.

First Printing, July, 1988

Library of Congress Cataloging in Publication Data

International Standard Book No. 0-87425-066-8

Composition by The Magazine Group
Wordprocessing by Susan Kotzin

Dedicated to Youth Everywhere
Who Are Reaching Out to Help Others
and by Doing So Are Making a Difference

Other Books by Sharon Scott

How to Say No and Keep Your Friends
Peer Pressure Reversal
Positive Peer Groups

About the Author

Sharon Scott is a licensed professional counselor, president of Sharon Scott and Associates, an international lecturer, and a frequent national and local radio and television talk show guest. Her Dallas-based firm offers training and consulting services to schools, social service agencies, religious groups, law enforcement agencies, and parent and youth groups.

She is also the author of three other books, *Peer Pressure Reversal, How to Say No and Keep Your Friends,* and *Positive Peer Groups.* She was honored with the Professional Writing Award by the Texas Association for Counseling and Development in 1987 and with a Certificate of Appreciation by Texas Governor Bill Clements in 1982.

Ms. Scott has taught more than a hundred thousand youth and adults in peer pressure reversal skills and developed numerous positive peer groups in school districts nationwide. She is past director of the Dallas Police Department's First Offender Program, which became a national model for delinquency prevention.

She has a master's degree in Human Relations and Community Affairs and over three hundred fifty hours of postgraduate work. She is featured in "Like a Roaring Lion," a video presentation about managing negative peer pressure.

In her free time, Ms. Scott loves to travel (especially to Africa), snow ski, and play with her three dogs.

Preface

We read and hear so much about negative peer pressure and how to deal with it and that is a very important issue. Many of you, however, have already learned how to manage such pressure and are open to bigger and better things. That is where this book comes in. I have written it to show you how to make more friends and also how to be helpful to the friends you have. This book is about thinking and acting positively, and about reaching out to help others.

Our nation is going through a time when material objects are overly important. You have to be "in"—or you are nobody. This generation has been called the ME generation, yet I think that with some hard work it could be, instead, the WE generation. We are dependent on one another for friendship and for love, both of which we all want.

When I went to school, it was good to make good grades, to not drink alcohol, to attend school (we used to try to go all year without missing a day), to be nice to lonely people, and to have projects to help those less fortunate than we were. Now in many places you are called a "brain" if you are a good student, a "chicken" if you do not drink alcohol, a "nerd" if you do not skip class, a "geek" if you talk to unpopular people, and a "wimp" if you try to help others. That is wrong; it is the reverse of the way it should be. Let's get back to common decency and learning to care about ourselves as well as others. I hope that is what you get out of *When to Say Yes!*

I would like to thank Dr. Robert R. Carkhuff for suggesting the title of this book and reviewing the program skills. It is from his classic book, *The Art of Helping,* that I designed the section of this book that deals with communicating with others. I appreciate the insightful editorial comments of Christopher Carkhuff. I also want to thank the following students who made suggestions on my rough draft and edited the manuscript to help give it a youthful perspective: John Parkin, grade 11; Tracy Kimbrough, grade 12; Kelly Kimbrough, grade 10; Jason Duncan, grade 7; and Sally McCall, grade 6. I also want to thank the thousands of students who have been a part of the positive peer groups I have developed in their schools, for I learned as much from them as I hope they did from me.

March 1988 Sharon Scott
Dallas, Texas

CONTENTS

Introduction: Peer Pressure Reversal 1

Phase 1: Make More Friends 13

Phase 2: Join a Group 41

Phase 3: Make Things Happen 65

Summary 91

Appendixes 101

INTRODUCTION: PEER PRESSURE REVERSAL

This book is about how to bring out the best in yourself and in others. But, first, examine yourself. In the past three months, have you:
- been called to the principal's office?
- sneaked out of the house at night with friends?
- gotten into a fistfight?
- been afraid to let friends know you made a good grade for fear others would call you a brain or nerd?
- used alcohol or other drugs?
- skipped classes to be with friends?
- lied to your parents about where you were going?
- thrown away a new outfit because friends did not like it?
- let someone copy your homework?
- stolen something while out with friends?
- driven fast to impress others?

These situations and many others like them are examples of negative peer pressure. What is negative peer pressure? It is the encouragement by others close to your age to try to get you to do something wrong with them. If you answered yes to any of the above questions, then you are probably not ready for the When to Say Yes! program.

WHEN TO SAY YES!

The bottom line is that if you cannot say no to your friends when necessary, then you cannot bring out the best in others, because you are not yet bringing out the best in yourself. You cannot be helpful to others because you are not a good role model for them.

So, for those of you who need to strengthen your decision-making skills, first obtain my book **How to Say No and Keep Your Friends.** Read it carefully; learn that you can still be popular while making wise choices for yourself. Study it. Put the lessons into practice, and then come back to this book to learn how to use positive peer pressure.

If you answered no to the list of questions outlining negative peer pressure situations, you should begin learning more about the When to Say Yes! program.

PEER PRESSURE REVERSAL

The When to Say Yes! program was designed to teach you to use positive peer pressure to make more friends and bring out the best in yourself and others. It can improve your attitude, make you happier, and allow you to have more fun—and help others do the same!

It has a lot to do with pride—in yourself, your friends, your school, the community where you live—and, in the end, even in your nation. If you truly take this book seriously, you can have a good impact on the world, because you will be more confident when standing up for what is good and right in yourself and others.

Debi Thomas, the twenty-year-old U.S. figure skater who competed in the 1988 Winter Olympics, is a perfect example of the When to Say Yes type. As a young girl she became fascinated with skating after she saw a show featuring the comedy skaters Frick and Frack. There followed years of costly lessons, driving long distances to practice, and tiring daily practices (even while she was a pre-med student in college). Not always having the funds for expensive costumes, she often sewed the tiny beads and sequins on her costumes. She worked hard to become the 1986 world champion skater.

In the 1988 Winter Olympics, she was once again competing with Katarina Witt, who had won the gold medal at the 1984 winter Olympics. Debi was leading as they were going into the final segment. But she had several slips, and instead of winning the gold, she received the bronze (third place) medal.

Is she a loser? Not at all! She is a winner all the way—because she **tried.**

After her performance, she said, "I still know I can do it. I just didn't do it at the right time." She added, "I'm still alive. I've got to get on with my life. Well, it's back to school. **At least I tried.**" Debi said yes to herself and became a winner. Now she is going back to college with plans to become an orthopedic surgeon. She will then be reaching out to help others. What a champion—in so many ways!

The When to Say Yes! program will allow you to express your sensitivity, to be caring, to share, to grow—and not to feel embarrassed by showing such feelings. We all feel pressured to "not get involved." If you do get involved, you try not to let anyone know about the good things you do, for fear that you will be teased. To be good or to do good should **not** be something that causes us to be ashamed.

Over the years I have been in numerous situations that involved helping something or someone. Occasionally I am teased about being a do-gooder or being very sentimental. I have learned not to give such comments even a second thought. I know that my actions were good, and I am proud of them.

In my first job after college, I was working in an office when a mentally ill person came in looking for his girlfriend, who worked there as a secretary. He had been drinking; he had a gun and planned to kill her. We all hid in our offices and tried to get as many people as we could from the halls to hide with us in the offices where we would be less likely to get shot. I was crouching under my desk with a very old man whom I had to help get down on the floor so he could get under the desk for protection. Fortunately, the police arrived and were able to talk the armed man into giving up his gun. We were all safe; we all had helped each other.

My husband and I were eating dinner in a restaurant in Washington, D.C., when out the window we saw a lady jogging with her two dogs. Suddenly, a stray dog came from nowhere and attacked her dogs. As her dogs tried to get away, one bolted into the street and was hit by a car. My husband and I ran out of the restaurant, leaving our food. We stopped traffic on that busy street to help the woman. My husband calmed her and helped her get her injured dog off the street. I ran after her smaller dog, who was so scared it had started to run wild. I finally caught up with it about eight blocks away. We helped the lady get home and then to the vet to get the injured dog treated.

I pick up so many stray dogs that my friends jokingly accuse me of picking up dogs from their front yards, dogs that are actually not lost. I have always gotten these scared stray animals back to their owners—or, in a few cases, to a new home.

On a business trip to Houston recently, I saw a drunk pedestrian on the busy freeway. As I watched, he fell facedown on the freeway and lay there. I yelled for the driver of the car I was in to stop, and we both ran down the middle of the freeway waving cars over so they would not hit the man. We finally got to him and helped drag him to the shoulder of the freeway. Someone called the police, and they soon arrived to assist.

Things like this happen all the time. Each one of us has got to decide whether we are going to sit back and not get involved or do what is right and help others, and in this way stand up for what we believe in. If we become so afraid of what someone else might say about our actions that we are stopped from doing what we know to be right, we are letting others control our thoughts and actions. And that is, basically, allowing someone else to control who we are.

Recently, a Dallas police officer, John Chase, made a routine traffic stop during heavy downtown traffic. While he was sitting in his patrol car checking information with headquarters, a stranger approached and began yelling at the officer to leave the citizen he had stopped alone. The officer told the man to go away, but the man refused. When the officer got out of his car to talk to the person he had stopped, he was verbally and then physically attacked by the intruding stranger. During the scuffle, the attacker got the officer's gun and shot him. As he walked away from the stricken officer, a few people waiting at the bus stop across the street cruelly yelled, "Shoot him again." This crazy man went back and put two more bullets in the officer's head. The 23-year-old officer, who was only doing his job protecting everyone, was killed. Sadly, no one came to the aid of the officer. How many people would it have taken to distract the man to give the officer a second to gain control of the situation? Only one—but there was not one.

I hope that this book motivates you, excites you, and encourages you to have the confidence to do what seems right to you and to help your friends to do the same.

WHEN TO SAY YES!

There are three sets of skills in the When to Say Yes! program. These skills will help you to COMMUNICATE interest to others, REINFORCE the positive in yourself and others, and SUPPORT the best in one another. These skills will help you to make more friends, join groups, and unite with others to make good things happen.

Table 1 shows that in Phase I you Make More Friends by **caring, pairing,** and **sharing**. In Phase II you Join a Group by **understanding, praising,** and **contributing** to your peers. In Phase III you Make Things Happen by using the following steps: **goal setting, guiding,** and **networking.**

I will follow discussions of each of these nine steps with two **true** stories—one to illustrate poor use of each step, and the other to give an example of its good use. All stories involve real people whom I have counseled, though their names have been changed to respect their privacy.

Table 1
WHEN TO SAY YES! PROGRAM

	COMMUNICATE	**REINFORCE**	**SUPPORT**
Phase I Make More Friends	Caring	Pairing	Sharing
Phase II Join a Group	Understanding	Praising	Contributing
Phase III Make Things Happen	Goal Setting	Guiding	Networking

10

Your generation has been called the ME generation, a term that describes this generation as a self-centered, selfish, and what's-in-it-for-me group. To some extent, that is an accurate description not only of **your** generation, but of much of the rest of today's society in general, because nowadays people have become overly concerned with money, being "in," status, and material possessions such as designer labels, fancy cars, and jewelry. Your generation has learned these attitudes from adults and from some of the media that glamorize such qualities.

However, from working with thousands of students in schools across the United States and in Canada, I am convinced that members of your generation are not just concerned about themselves, but about their friends and fellow students, too. More and more of our youth are reaching out as individuals and through groups to help each other. Most of them understand that happiness does not come through material possessions, but from one's relationships with others. More and more young people are showing that they have the guts and the smarts to say no to alcohol and other drugs, and to feel that they have the right and the responsibility to help others do the same.

In other words, I feel that your generation is not the ME generation but the WE generation! So many of you want to make a difference and are making a difference! Your generation is fed up with the unbelievably high rates of teenage drug use, pregnancy, crime, and the school drop-out rate. The suicide rate of teenagers is the highest in any generation. Your generation can bring

WHEN TO SAY YES!

about changes that can have a positive effect not only in your lifetime but far beyond. We can wipe out many of these problems if we learn to **communicate** with, **reinforce**, and **support** each other! There are groups in schools across the nation that are already demonstrating the effects of the When to Say Yes! program. Later, we will learn more about some of these groups—SWAT, STAR, STOP, TRY, TAD, STARS, H_2O, and even the NURDS. Now let's learn When to Say Yes.

PHASE I: MAKE MORE FRIENDS

MAKE MORE FRIENDS

The objective of Phase I is to make more friends—"The more, the merrier," it is often said. Some of you may feel lonely, as if you have no friends. Others of you may think you have quite a few friends but could use more. And some of you may think that your friends are not true-blue—not really loyal. Or maybe there are some really bad characters in your group who often get you into trouble, and you know, deep down, that you need some new friends. It can be scary to think of making or changing friends. We all fear rejection by someone new. When we try to change from one kind of friend to another, we worry what will happen in between as we give up our old friends and take up with the new ones. Many people stay with a boy or girl friend whom they no longer like because they don't know what to do with themselves until they find some new boy or girl to become friends with. First of all, you must realize that nothing terribly bad will happen during that time.

For example, I did not find anyone I wanted to marry until I was age thirty-one. During many years of dating I changed and added many friends, as I dated a lot of different men. I learned that there may be times when there are too many guys interested in you at one time—and there may also be times when no one is interested. You have to go with the flow and not feel insecure if there is no member of the opposite sex constantly in the picture.

I also changed girlfriends a lot during those years. Some of my close friends got married in their early twenties and either moved away or spent most of their time with their new husbands. As time went on, some became mothers and had even less free time. We remained friends, but our interests had gone in different directions, and we saw less of each other. We kept in touch but mainly by telephone, Christmas cards, and an occasional lunch. So I had to keep seeking new friends.

We will learn how to reach out and make more friends by using the **caring, pairing,** and **sharing** steps. In **caring,** you learn to pay attention to others, so that you can select appropriate friends. In **pairing,** you learn what to do to begin a friendship. And in **sharing,** you learn to appreciate, respect, and share your life's experiences. In the Make More Friends phase, you will learn the true value of healthy relationships.

During my single years, I had a friend named Elaine who had just been through a difficult divorce. One day while visiting her, I tried to talk her into doing things together with me, like playing tennis, walking our dogs, going to the store—**anything** to meet some new people (especially guys!). I recall that she did not want to do anything; the very thought of meeting someone new made her nervous. I jokingly said that she couldn't expect new friends to come and ring her doorbell. Right at that moment her doorbell rang! We looked at each other and laughed. It was a new neighbor, asking to borrow a cup of milk—and he was very handsome. When he left, Elaine said, "I told you new friends would show up." I said he was probably cooking dinner for his girlfriend. Within five minutes, he was back, and with him was an even better looking male friend! They invited us to have dinner with them. We had a good time as we shared the hamburgers that the two men had cooked on the grill. Elaine ended up dating her neighbor for over a year.

The point of this story, though, is that this kind of good fortune is **rare**! Realize that new friends do not just appear at your doorstep. You have to make an effort to gain new friends.

The first step in Phase I is **caring**—about yourself and about others. In order to care about others, you must first care about yourself.

This means several things: dressing neatly and in clothes appropriate for the occasion, cleanliness, a good sense of humor, courtesy, standing tall, and a positive self-concept.

Dressing neatly and appropriately for the occasion means that your clothes should be clean and pressed; your clothes should complement you. Don't stand out by wearing outrageous clothing suitable only for Halloween. Such clothing will get attention, but the wrong kind. As a counselor I have heard time after time teenagers telling me that they dress in weird outfits to shock others or to get attention. These people usually lack self-confidence and are unable to determine positive ways to get attention.

Cleanliness is part of **caring** since it shows that you know your body image is important. Bathe or shower daily; use a deodorant and, if you like, a light touch of perfume or cologne.

A good sense of humor means that you must have the ability to smile, laugh, and see funny things in life. Humor should not be used to put others down—yet, sadly, it often is. Don't laugh at that kind of humor; try to change the subject to something positive. A sense of humor also means the ability to laugh at yourself. I do that a lot! Speaking frequently as I do to large groups of people, I have been known to say words backwards or trip on a microphone cord. Once I even fell off a stage. But each time my ability to laugh heartily at these episodes allowed the audience to relax and laugh without embarrassing anyone. It helps to avoid appearing to be stuck-up.

Courtesy is being thoughtful in various ways, such as sending birthday or congratulation cards, helping someone pick up dropped books, throwing trash in a trash can (even if someone else dropped it), being nice to your brothers' and sisters' friends, and letting your parents know where you are going and when you will be home (if you do this yourself first, they won't give you the third degree as you leave). There are unlimited ways to express courtesy. The important thing to realize is that the more you show courtesy, the more often it will be returned to you.

Standing tall is very important in making new friends. It shows that you are interested in others, and it is the initial move toward a friendship. Your body posture sends an immediate message to others: either "Hi, I'm friendly," or "I'm shy—don't talk to me." If you walk down the hall in school with your books tightly held in front of you and your head down, you do not look friendly. You look too serious, as though you are not interested in meeting anyone. Instead, do these three things: stand tall, hold your books to your side, and make eye contact as you walk along. If someone looks back at you, smile. If you stop to talk, stand directly in front of the person and keep eye contact. The person you are speaking with should be your center of attention. If you give others this kind of quality attention, then they are more likely to give attention back to you. Look at the picture in Figure 1. Which person are you more likely to want to talk to? Obviously, the person on the right. Practice this; it really works!

MAKE MORE FRIENDS

WHEN TO SAY YES!

Positive self-concept means that you think you can succeed, and therefore you try. You believe in yourself. Most things that you learn will not be accomplished the first time you try. Mistakes are only practices! And we know that practice makes perfect. Well, it may not always make us perfect, but we can become good at things. I learned to snow ski nine years ago. I was ready to give up on day one, and day two, and even day three; but I knew I would never learn to ski if I did. Guess what? After **lots** of mistakes (remember, they are just practices), on day four I was skiing okay. And I keep getting better. A beginning skier recently asked me if I ever fall anymore. I told her yes, definitely; I would not be improving my skiing if I did not fall. If I ski very carefully, I will not fall, but neither will I improve. Don't be afraid to try—to raise your hand in class to give an answer, to ask a girl for a date, to give a chemical-free party (yes, people will come), and to really study and try for a good grade.

There is nothing wrong in being nervous when you try something new. That happens to all of us. But there is something wrong in saying "I'm not going to try" or, worse, "I can't do it." Both sentences express an attitude that totally defeats you **before** you even begin.

Remember, none of us is good at all things. We all have strengths as well as weaknesses. I am good at snow skiing, photography, and public speaking because I have practiced those things. I'm not so good at math, swimming, or sewing, but I still try to improve. I do the best that I can, which is all that any of us can do. We may have natural abilities in some areas. My natural abilities do not lie in singing, for example, but that does not keep me from singing. I know that is not one of my best skills, but I know I am strong in others. In other words, don't compare yourself with others. Be yourself—do what you are good at, and be proud of it.

I know of a seventh-grade boy who was very talented at playing the piano. In fact, he was so good it probably could have become his profession. He loved to play, but he gave it up in junior high because he thought guys his age should play sports, not a piano. He let others control his self-esteem and did not appreciate his own individual qualities.

WHEN TO SAY YES!

The following items, taken from two "Dear Abby" columns, are about famous people who managed to succeed against the odds, either physical or mental. If these people had thought "I can't do it," you know that these achievements would never have been made.

Amputate the cancer-ridden leg of a handsome, young Canadian, and you have a Terry Fox, who vowed to run on one leg across Canada to raise a million dollars for cancer research. (Terry was forced to quit halfway when cancer invaded his lungs, but he managed to raise about $20 million.)

Tell a young boy who loved to sketch and draw that he has no talent, and you have a Walt Disney.

At birth, deny a child the ability to see, hear, and speak, and you have a Helen Keller.

Strike a young man down with infantile paralysis, and you have a Franklin D. Roosevelt, the only president of the United States to be elected to four terms.

Label a person "too stupid to learn," and you have a Thomas Edison.

Call a child dull and hopeless and flunk him in sixth grade, and you have a Winston Churchill.

Have an infant born black in a society filled with racial discrimination, and you have a Booker T. Washington, Harriet Tubman, Marian Anderson, George Washington Carver, or Martin Luther King, Jr.

Call a boy a slow learner, retarded, and write him off as uneducable, and you have an Albert Einstein.

If someone in your life, including yourself, is telling you that "you can't," please know you can. Say yes to yourself!

An Example of Poor Caring

Jennifer was in eighth grade in a new school because her mother had remarried and the family had moved across town. She had always done well in school. She had an interest in horseback riding, and she and her horse had been in competition for the past five years. She had dreams of going to national competition with her horse. She was depressed after her parents' divorce and had never really accepted her stepfather. She blamed the move on him.

It is difficult to begin a new school, for we are unsure what it will be like and yet we all want to be accepted. Jennifer's way to show others that she cared about them was share their values: to dress just like them (this group always wore all black) and accept dares to show off. Unfortunately, the crowd she had chosen to impress was one that had an I-don't-care attitude. This group hated school; they were using drugs and were very rebellious. Jennifer began cutting classes; her grades quickly dropped to C's and F's. She lost interest in riding and even quit going to the stables to feed and care for her horse. At first, her parents took over these chores, but finally they sold the horse. They then grounded Jennifer when they discovered that she had been shoplifting with her friends. She complained to her boyfriend, whom she had just met on the very day that her parents had punished her. They decided to run away together. Jennifer was arrested. Her dreams were shattered.

Jennifer's experience is an example of poor **caring** about yourself and others.

An Example of Good Caring

Tina, like Jennifer, had been through some rough years with her family. Her parents had divorced and had had a lengthy court battle over her custody. Both parents wanted her to live with them, and she was too young at the time to be involved in the decision. She was now beginning the sixth grade in her fourth elementary school in four years. Her mother had remarried, and there was a new baby in the family. Tina was not sure if she was really loved at home. So much family fighting had lowered her self-esteem.

But as she eagerly began counseling, she expressed hopes of making new friends and letting go of the past. She wanted to care about herself again and began working on how to stand tall. She had a lovely smile and tried to show it more. At first, she used to make negative comments about herself, such as "I'm stupid" or "I can't do that." But she learned that such an attitude would not help her self-esteem.

One day she wrote me a note that said, "Smile, be friendly, be helpful, look good, be a leader, get involved, be enthusiastic! 'YUCK!'—that is what I **used** to would have said. But **now** I say, 'I'll do my best, because the harder you try, the easier it is to do better.' "

During our last conversation, she told me that she now understands others in ways that she never even thought she could. She said she has lots of friends now—one of them was even a person that she had never really liked!

Tina made a lot of changes. But her learning to care about herself allowed her to learn to care about others.

The second step in Phase I is **pairing**, which is to meet a person who might become a new friend. The first step in meeting a new person is selecting someone to meet, then greeting that person. After introductions are made, the talk (and a potential friendship) can begin.

In selecting someone you'd like to get to know, be sure to note the qualities of the person. If he or she does well in school, has a good attitude, follows rules at home and in the community, and does not use alcohol or other drugs, then he or she has the potential of being a quality friend. If the person does not meet these standards, then he or she could easily be a trouble friend.

Where do you look for friends? They could be anywhere—in class, in the cafeteria, in clubs or other organizations, in your neighborhood, in a religious youth group, or on athletic teams. Don't defeat yourself with negative thinking such as "That person probably wouldn't like me" or "I don't like anyone in my school. They are all stuck up." That kind of thinking will not help you reach your goal.

WHEN TO SAY YES!

Once you have selected someone you would like to meet, the next step in **pairing** is greeting. A greeting has five parts: approach the person; say hello; introduce yourself; engage in some chit-chat; and invite him or her to an appropriate activity. Approach potential friends at a time when you can talk to them. This might be either when they are alone or when they are in light conversation with others and you see an open place among them that you can properly fill. (See figure 2. Note that the group on the bottom would be easier to approach.)

Then make your approach by walking up to the person or the group. Smile. When someone turns to look at you, say, "Hi," or "Hello," and introduce yourself: "I'm _____[your name]_____." Then participate in some casual conversation, the kind I call chit-chat. If anyone neglects to tell you his or her name, ask. Then you can talk about classes, where you are from, your hobbies or interests, where you live, Friday's game, or anything like that. This may be difficult to do at first, but the rewards will be worth it!

MAKE MORE FRIENDS

GROUP IS "CLOSED"

GROUP IS "OPEN"

31

An Example of Poor Pairing

Andy was a ninth-grader who had not done well in school. His parents knew he had potential and recently had enrolled him in a private school known for motivating students. He knew no one at this new school, but he wanted friends. Being tall and husky for his age, he sought friends among the older kids and was frustrated when they would not accept him. Andy didn't drive, date, or have a part-time job like some of the eleventh- and twelfth-graders he wanted to hang around with. He could not understand that he did not have enough in common with them to be accepted as a friend.

His parents encouraged him to get involved in school activities so he could meet friends his age. He tried out for football, but quit the third day because he got too hot. He joined the band, but decided that people that played any instrument other than the drums were nerds. He also tried out for basketball, but quit when he got put on the B team because of his lack of experience. When he was urged to get a part-time job, he said that he would accept nothing except a sales clerk's position at an expensive clothing store. So he had no job.

Andy did not take the correct steps for **pairing**. He was lonely, mad at the world. Eventually he got accepted by an older, drug-using group. When his parents tried to help, he ran away from home. He was arrested for running away and as a minor in possession of alcohol. Eventually his parents placed him in a boys' home.

An Example of Good Pairing

Joe was in the eleventh grade and had dreams of going to college. Because of his father's occupation, his family had moved a lot in his lifetime. He had about given up trying to make friends because he said as soon as he would make them the family would move again.

During counseling sessions he told me how lonely he was. He wanted not only to have male friends but also to have a date. Going through the steps of **pairing**, he thought of three guys and two girls as possible friends. He saw them often in school and in Sunday school. One was a newcomer in the neighborhood. He introduced himself to a quiet guy at school and suggested having lunch together. They found they had a lot in common, and have become good friends. He played touch football with the other two guys. Before long, he learned that they liked to do mean pranks and engage in vandalism, so he decided not to continue those relationships. The first girl he asked out, a popular cheerleader, politely turned him down. The second girl accepted, and they have been dating for a long time.

Joe has continued the **pairing** steps and continues to add to his circle of friends.

If the initial conversation upon meeting goes well, then you may ask if the person would like to join you in some such activity as a soft drink after school, a movie, a tennis match, lunch, or a study session together. This is the **sharing** step of Phase I. Plan the time, day, and location, since your objective is to get to know each other by **sharing** a planned event. If, however, the conversation runs short the first time, you might decide to plan a get-together during your second conversation.

Some people get nervous thinking about greeting someone new. What is the worst thing that can happen? The worst thing that can happen is that your conversation will be just fair—not great. Big deal! You can live with that. Bear in mind that the other person may be shy, and the conversation may begin slowly. I have had many conversations like that—conversations that later led to good friendships.

As you continue to see your new friend, you can both be more open; you can express your real feelings, dreams, and ideas. In the beginning, it is appropriate to share small pieces of yourself. This gives you time to check whether your new friend is loyal to you, can keep personal information confidential, and truly cares about you. **Sharing** everything about yourself too early is usually not good, for it moves the friendship too quickly, at the risk of becoming emotionally costly.

As you continue to exchange life experiences, you will be supporting one another. At times, you will share solutions to problems. But most important, always be there for each other.

An Example of Poor Sharing

In tenth grade, Jackie fell madly in love with an eleventh-grade guy named Greg. Jackie was sensitive, emotional, and expressed herself well in writing. In notes and letters to Greg, she wrote about personal problems of her family, her love for him, and her hopes for their future together. Within two months of their first meeting, their relationship came to a halt. In fact, they had such a bad disagreement that they called each other names and put each other down every chance they could get.

Jackie was depressed about their breakup but tried to have a good attitude and go about her way. Greg, however, held a grudge. He made xerox copies of Jackie's letters and passed them around the school to embarrass her.

Jackie learned too late about **sharing**. She had shared too much too soon.

An Example of Good Sharing

Nick was in his first year of college, eager to do well and to meet people. He made many excellent efforts in **sharing**. He belonged to the Business Club and invited several members to have a soft drink with him after one of their meetings. Over soft drinks, they talked about a common interest—business. Their informal gatherings became regular events, and he expanded the conversations each time to share more about himself and learn more about his new friends.

Nick often saw an attractive girl playing tennis as he walked across campus. One day the ball came over the fence as he was walking by. He took that opportunity to greet her. The following week he stopped and watched the game. She smiled at him. When the game ended, Nick jokingly asked for a lesson. She said, "Anytime." Nick quickly arranged a time for their tennis date. This was the beginning of a good friendship that lasted all his college years.

WHEN TO SAY YES!

Think about what you have learned in Phase I. Discuss and share these ideas—they are valuable tools. Now go out and make a new friend. Use this worksheet as a guide.

1. List several people whom you might try to develop into friends:

   _____
   _____
   _____
   _____

2. Pick one of them to begin with. Decide on how to approach that person.

   _____

3. As you greet him or her, have in mind some topics of mutual interest for a casual conversation. The topics could be:

   _____
   _____
   _____
   _____

4. What activity do you plan to invite your new acquaintance to share with you? _____
   When? _____
   Where? _____
   Don't put this off! Do it this week! And enjoy the benefits; you deserve them.

MAKE MORE FRIENDS

REMEMBER:

CARING
PAIRING
SHARING

LEADS TO MAKING MORE FRIENDS!

PHASE 2: JOIN A GROUP

Have you ever needed someone to talk to and had no one? Or have you ever tried to discuss a problem with people who say, "Sorry about that," then turn things around by asking your advice on matters troubling them? You end up helping them solve their problems instead of getting help yourself! Have you ever felt that people your age are not capable of real sensitivity and sharing of feelings? I hear such complaints all the time.

In Phase II, you will learn to Join a Group, so that you can support its members and the group can support you. You will learn steps called **understanding, praising,** and **contributing**.

In **understanding** you learn how to communicate effectively. **Praising** teaches you to reinforce positive things in yourself and others—to encourage, to think, and to reward positive thoughts, and to act upon them. In **contributing** you learn that to give, you receive. Phase II allows you and your friends to become support systems for each other.

Step 1, **understanding**, is the ability to **really** hear and feel what the other person is telling you. You are in the conversation fully. You pay attention, listen well, and "see the world through the other person's eyes."

Understanding has two parts: communicating what you hear the other person is saying and communicating to them your impression of how they feel. This lays a base for caring about the feelings of others and communicating that to them.

JOIN A GROUP

To communicate **understanding**, you must first accurately hear what the other person is saying. It helps you to be clear about the information that you are receiving. It requires that you say the word "you" more often than the word "I." This, too, helps us to move from the ME generation to the WE generation. You can use this format to practice:

You're saying _____.

Fill in the blank by rephrasing briefly what you heard the other person say.

WHEN TO SAY YES!

The second part of **understanding** is the ability to communicate to the other person that you sincerely understand how he or she feels. How others feel causes them to act in certain ways, leading to a real understanding of others. You can use this format to practice:

You feel _____.

To become more accurate in words that describe feeling, add to the list in table 2 to expand your "feeling" vocabulary. In other words, fill in the blanks of a column with words having meanings similar to that of the word at the top of the column.

Table 2

HAPPY	SAD	MAD	SCARED	CONFUSED	WEAK	STRONG
good	down	furious	nervous	mixed up	unsure	powerful
excited	lonely	irritated	uptight	lost	used	sure
___	___	___	___	___	___	___
___	___	___	___	___	___	___
___	___	___	___	___	___	___

You have to really look at and listen to others closely to understand accurately how those persons feel.

Now let's put these formats together into a high level of **understanding**—stating back to others that you understand how they feel and why they feel that way. The complete communication statement would be:

You're saying _____ and that makes you feel _____.

Here is a completed worksheet by a former client of mine who had completed his practice of **understanding**.

You're saying *that 95* on that test makes you feel great.
You're saying *the way Mark is treating you* makes you feel *angry*.
You're saying *your sister is having a lot of problems* and that makes you feel *concerned.*
You're saying *you've never been to Utah and you're looking forward to the visit* and you're *excited.*
You're saying that *your teacher believes you care about this class* and that makes you *happy.*

My client actually said these sentences to his friends in order to communicate his **understanding**. He reported to me that in each case his friend was made to feel that he really cared, and they ended up talking more in depth on each subject. He said that using this skill allowed him to get closer to people.

Here is a worksheet for you to fill in. Practice your making your statement of **understanding** with at least one person a day to get in the habit of using it.

You're saying _____
_____ and that makes you feel _____.

You're saying _____
_____ and that makes you feel _____.

You're saying _____
_____ and that makes you feel _____.

You're saying _____
_____ and that makes you feel _____.

You're saying _____
_____ and that makes you feel _____.

You're saying _____
_____ and that makes you feel _____.

You're saying _____
_____ and that makes you feel _____.

An Example of Poor Understanding

Mike was a junior in high school. He had had the same group of friends since elementary school and had added no others. He was quiet and serious and tried to understand people by just being a good listener. He rarely had anything to say in return, so conversations with him were short. He said he had thoughts to express, but he thought so long on what to say and exactly how to say it that the other person would begin talking, finally end the conversation, and then walk off. Mike was frustrated by his inability to communicate understanding to others and by this means to let them know he was interesting as well as interested.

WHEN TO SAY YES!

An Example of Good Understanding

   Shawn was a senior looking forward to graduating, and he hoped to go to college. A good student, he was worried about being too quiet. He had never had a date because he did not know what to say. He felt that he knew his parents and brother well because they all talked a lot, but did not think they knew him that well because he had trouble carrying on conversations. He also knew that if he was to do well in the business world, he must learn to communicate better.
   So Shawn enrolled in a course at a community college that was open to the public. The course was called Communicating with Confidence. In that course, he learned to hear what others were saying, to understand how they were feeling, and to communicate that understanding to them by saying, "You're saying _____ and that makes you feel _____ ." In fact, the worksheet on page 47 is a copy of one of his assignments.
   Shawn has had many dates since then. He has graduated from college and is a successful young man. His ability to communicate better has enabled him to get further in life—and to feel deeply.

50

The second step of Phase II, Join a Group, is **praising**. It is my favorite step. Being positive, looking on the bright side, giving compliments, noticing the good are all important parts of getting along with others. It can help you to like yourself and enables you to show others that you care about them. You have to really work at this step, for we are daily bombarded by negatives: the headlines of newspapers scream about the latest war, accident, or death; one brand of toothpaste (or deodorant, or blue jeans, or any other product) puts the other brands down; we rush through our days with no time to "stop and smell the roses"; a lot of music and television programs are about violence, illicit love affairs, materialism, and getting drunk. It sometimes seems your parents expect you to be perfect, when everything around you seems faulty. No wonder we get negative.

Sometimes you do things well and no one notices, or everyone is too busy to say anything. Yet when you do something wrong, everyone always seems to notice. What is even worse is when you do something well and others put you down for it. For example, you make a good grade and someone sneers, "You're so smart. You never have to study. I'm just glad I'm not a bookworm." Wouldn't it have been nice if someone had just said, "Hey, good grade"?

It is important to understand that you cannot give sincere praise to others if you don't like yourself. You cannot give something away that you do not have. You must first work on thinking positive thoughts about yourself on a regular basis.

When an airplane is taking off and the flight attendant gives instructions, he or she always says that should there be an emergency and oxygen is needed, adults are to put the mask on themselves **before** helping children put them on. Why? Without oxygen, the adult would be unable to help. In other words, you have to have oxygen before you can give it away. Too often we think negative things about ourselves: we do not like our looks, we feel we say dumb things, we do not make good-enough grades, and so on. This is a bad habit. It lowers our self-esteem; we must change such an attitude.

When you get a praising statement from another, do you ever put yourself down or take your accomplishment for granted? Replies like "This old thing?" when someone compliments you on your outfit, or "Anyone could do it" when a friend tells you that you did a job well, will do just that. Let us look at how to praise ourselves and others.

The parts to **praising** are:

1. Attend the person.
   Face the person, give eye contact, smile.

2. State what action it was that you liked.
   Be specific, use a phrase like "I noticed that _____."

3. Add praise words.
   Add those extra words we like to hear, like "Thanks," "I appreciate it," "Great."

4. Don't use put-downs.

   Nothing else needs to be said. Don't make it negative with a comparison such as "This is a lot better than last time," or "I didn't think you could do it."

   By **praising**, you make other persons feel good about themselves and the things they do. It helps friends to make constructive, healthy choices.

WHEN TO SAY YES!

An example of a **praising** statement to say to a friend might be:

> "I noticed you controlled your temper even when the other person wanted to fight. That took a lot of guts."

An example of **praise** to say to a parent might be:

> "Dad, you look sharp in your new shirt. It's a good color for you."

An example of a **praising** statement to say to a teacher might be:

> "Mrs. Cates, I appreciate your taking the time to explain this problem. It helped a lot."

An example of a **praising** thought about ourselves might be:

> "I noticed that I finished my homework before I turned the TV on. I'm glad I can be serious about my grades."

These are all just examples. The important thing is that you start giving more **praise** to others and yourself.

It is so important to get into the habit of thinking positive thoughts about yourselves that I want you to use table 3, on this page, to begin recording once each day something that you did or said that you are proud of. Once the page is full, get a notebook and continue noting in it each day a positive thought about yourself. This is not bragging (no one will see this but you); it is intended to help you establish a habit of thinking positively. The notebook can also be helpful when you get down on yourself, for you can look back on the many good things that you have said or done and think better of yourself.

Table 3
Positive Thoughts About Myself

Day 1 _____

Day 2 _____

Day 3 _____

Day 4 _____

Day 5 _____

Day 6 _____

Day 7 _____

An Example of Poor Praising

Brian had only one friend. He said that was fine with him, because he met few people that he really liked. He frequently had a scowl on his face, because he liked to look tough. He said that way other people would pick on him less. He never had a word of praise for anyone. In fact, he thought that noticing good things about others was "sissy stuff."

No wonder Brian had only one friend! Brian was actually afraid to be positive. He was not sure that others would like him, so he never gave them a chance—that way he avoided being hurt. He also avoided being liked.

An Example of Good Praising

With the last name of Wong, Sam was often teased by others who liked to make stupid rhymes using his name. It hurt at first, and he often hit people who did that, and called them names right back. As Sam and I talked, he realized that others often tease because of their insecurities and immaturity. By putting others down, some feel that they build themselves up.

So he decided to begin a positive attack on this problem. He commented when classmates made good grades, noticed others' new clothes, and just shook his head and laughed when he heard the rhymes using his name. Within a month the problem was solved, and Sam had become friends with many classmates. A teacher told his mother one day, "All the kids like Sam. He's just so positive about everything!" And to himself, Sam praised his efforts.

Praising others and yourself makes good sense.

WHEN TO SAY YES!

The third step in Phase II is **contributing**. Your objective is to join a group and act as a contributing member of that group. First you must find and join a group in your school or community.

Think of your interest areas and select accordingly. If you like to talk or express yourself, you might join the Speech or Drama Club. If you have strong feelings about helping others, become involved in Young Life or your school's antidrug group. The Newcomers' Club is appropriate for new students. There are many other groups to link up with such as the Scouts, the Youth Fellowship at a church or synagogue, Future Farmers of America, various boys' and girls' clubs, the YMCA, the YWCA, a swim team, or any of the activities sponsored by your local recreation or parks department.

You already know the skills needed to join a group; that goes back to **caring, pairing,** and **sharing**. If there are no groups to select from, you may want to start one yourself. In fact, you may even find yourself in a leader's role.

Once you are in a group, you will want to remember to use **understanding** and **praising** in your communication so that you add to the effectiveness of the group. Some people "take away" from a group with comments like "That won't work" or "No one will like that idea." Such useless comments are better not said. If you cannot contribute a better or different idea, then support others' ideas.

An Example of Poor Contributing

Shirley had difficulty making the transition from junior high to high school. There were a lot more people in high school, and she was not in classes with many people she knew. Overwhelmed by this situation, she would sometimes pretend to be sick so that she could avoid going to that place with all the strangers.

I talked with Shirley about joining a group so that she could feel she was a part of her school. She said it was a good idea, but she never seemed to know when the groups met or which one she wanted to join. She avoided taking any constructive action and was not helping herself.

When one is alone, things can be scary.

An Example of Good Contributing

George was a junior in high school but still did not feel that he was a part of the school. Most of the other kids had grown up together. He had moved into this school when he was in the ninth grade. He was involved in several school activities, but all the kids already seemed to be divided up into special groups of friends. As we talked one day, the possibility of his participating in the Newcomers' Club (because he still felt like a newcomer) was discussed.

When he checked into this with his counselor, he was surprised that his school did not have such a club. George decided to start one. He talked to several adults at school who tried to discourage him, since they felt that there were already enough clubs. He explained his feelings, saying that surely others felt as he did. These students, he said, needed to meet some new people and make friends. They would then feel more a part of the school. It took several months to find an adult sponsor, draft by-laws, and get word out about the club. Finally, the first meeting was held. Thirty students came, and George was elected president!

Being alone can be tough. The togetherness of a group can support us, energize everyone, and be a powerful force.

Phase I helped us in our individual relationships. Phase II has taught us how to be both helpful and helped in group situations. **Understanding** helps you communicate fully. **Praising** helps you bring out the best in others. **Contributing** helps you to work with others in healthy ways.

JOIN A GROUP

REMEMBER:

UNDERSTANDING
PRAISING
CONTRIBUTING

*LEAD TO JOINING
A GROUP!*

PHASE 3: MAKE THINGS HAPPEN

In Phase III, you will learn how to Make Things Happen—good and exciting things. This is where you can reach out and really help people. Good, healthy, caring relationships are what life is really about.

I recently read about a survey conducted by Dr. Kenneth Green at UCLA to find out what students think is important. Participants were given a list of goals, and each was asked to pick one or more of them that he or she thought was important.

Of those surveyed in 1967, more than two-thirds (68.7 percent) picked helping the less fortunate as one of the things they considered important. In contrast, making good money was one of the choices of less than half (42 percent) of them.

In twenty years, the emphasis had shifted. The same survey of a new generation of students in 1987 showed that making good money was one of the goals of more than three-quarters (75.6 percent) of them, while only a little more than half of them thought helping the less fortunate was important!

Do you see the change? Money—"me, myself, and I"—had increased in importance, as if money were the key to happiness!

WHEN TO SAY YES!

The key to happiness is one's relationships with others. In order to Make Things Happen, you will learn the following steps: **goal setting, guiding, and networking. In goal setting** you will learn how to identify goals. **Guiding** will teach you how to confront negative behavior and reinforce good behavior. And in **networking** you will learn to band together with other individuals or groups to achieve a common purpose or goal. This phase will help you focus your resources and efforts on the improvement of your school, neighborhood, community, and nation.

The first step of Phase III, **goal setting**, shows you how to take responsibility for individual or group goals. A goal is basically a clear understanding of where you or a group needs to be or wants to be.

In order to set goals, you must check out the scene around you. As an individual, use your eyes and your ears to notice if someone is being left out or is lonely, if someone is being teased unkindly, if someone is being asked to do something wrong, if a fight is being planned, and so on. You are trying to determine how, as an individual, you might offer help.

If your group is going to function as a **positive peer group**—one that actively works on improving the school—the members must discuss the problem areas that exist. Problems that some groups might want to tackle are alcohol or other drugs, truancy, gossip and cliques, loneliness, lack of school spirit, teen pregnancy, or reckless driving. The groups addressing such problems are not intended to be just social clubs but, rather, service groups that actively try to help others.

It is appropriate for you to have individual goals as well as to be a part of a positive peer group that aims for larger goals. Remember that you cannot work on numerous goals all at one time, because your efforts will become too scattered. You and the group should select only one or two goals to work on at a time. Select something of interest and meaningful as a goal.

For example, my two loves in volunteer work are working with the elderly and with animals. Therefore, I have set two goals for myself in this area. One is to visit a nursing home once a month with one of my dogs. This is an established program, sponsored by my local Society for the Prevention of Cruelty to Animals (SPCA). My cocker spaniel and I go from room to room chatting with the patients. Most of them love to see us and even remember the dog's name! Occasionally, I also help with some exhibit booths for the SPCA to provide humane education about pet care. I even visit the animal shelter, where I walk the dogs and pet the cats. This helps the animals to socialize and become more adoptable. Some have been mistreated or lost for a long time and need lots of tender, loving care. These two volunteer projects are not too time-consuming, and provide me and others with much joy and satisfaction.

Some examples of individual goals that could help others include:

Saying "Hi" to more people each day
Giving sincere praise to others
Really listening to others' problems
Introducing new students around
Eating lunch with someone who is alone
Quietly telling the person being criticized to ignore the comments and getting the person away from the teasing
Avoiding gossip
Doing volunteer work at a hospital, humane society, or nursing home
Other: _____
Other: _____

Record one or two individual goals that you intend to begin working on **now**.

1. _____
2. _____

Some examples of group goals to help others might include:

- Teaching other students in your school peer pressure reversal skills (remember, these techniques are outlined in my book *How to Say No and Keep Your Friends*)
- Sponsoring a Newcomers' Club
- Writing and producing a play about negative peer pressure
- Sponsoring an essay and art contest about how to handle difficult decisions, with prizes (donated by stores and restaurants) for the winners
- Presenting a program on the harmful effects of alcohol and other drugs
- Sponsoring "Meet Someone New at Lunch Day," when people entering the cafeteria can sit at color-coded tables (marked with balloons or streamers), breaking up the usual groups so that everyone has an opportunity to meet new people
- Volunteering before or after school as tutors
- Putting posters all over school about the harmful effects of alcohol and other drugs
- Having a guest speaker talk on how to have a fun party without alcohol or other drugs; entertainment ideas, games, and food; and how to make "mocktails" (see appendix 1 for recipes)—not cocktails
- Planning a big bash, without chemicals, for the graduating seniors

Getting business cards printed with your group's name and the message "Call me—I care" or "Call me if I can help" imprinted on them (be sure to leave spaces for the group member's name and phone number)

Helping start a parent-peer group

Discussing "truth in advertising"—or what ads and commercials do not tell us about products like tobacco and alcohol

Sponsoring in the school newspaper a Dear Abby-type column answering questions about teen life (have the school counselor assist with the answers)

Aligning your group with state or national youth organizations and raising funds to send representatives of your group to annual conferences of a state or national group

Add your ideas. By listening to the creative ideas of group members, you will come up with lots of ideas. List some that come to mind now:

1. _____
2. _____

An Example of Poor Goal Setting

One school that decided to start a positive peer group got together a group of the most popular youngsters, who, selected officers, chose a name, and then began discussing goals! Each person tried to have his or her idea be adopted. There was little listening and no understanding. The members critized each idea, saying, "That won't work." Out of frustration they adjourned the meeting, and when they tried to set a date for the next meeting, no one could find a convenient time; all said they were too busy.

These were some of the mistakes they made:

 They did not select members that represented a cross-section of the student body.
 There was no need for officers. This was not to be a social club, but a team effort dedicated to helping others.
 The skills of **caring, understanding,** and **praising** were not used.
 These people were too busy with other things to be serious participants in a positive peer group.

An Example of Good Goal Setting

In Ball High School, Galveston, Texas, 150 students were so interested in developing a positive peer group that they gave up two full days of summer vacation in August to meet with me to be trained. They were concerned because, during the eighteen months prior to the training, seven Ball High School students had died. The causes of death included suicide, drowning, and traffic accidents. Alcohol and other drugs were involved in some of the incidents.

These youths were determined. They represented a cross section of the student body and included more than 5 percent of the total school enrollment. There were definitely enough of them to really Make Things Happen.

After much brainstorming, we focused on action plans, five major problems stood out: alcohol and other drugs; truancy; gossip and cliques; teen pregnancy; and the dress code. The 150 students met in five teams of roughly thirty participants each to address each problem.

Galveston is an island community off the Gulf Coast of Texas. Because of its location and its goals, the group called itself H_2O—Help to Others!

In the next step of Phase III, you will become better equipped in **guiding** your goals or the group's goal toward completion. It is not enough just to have great ideas or good intentions; you must move to act on your goals.

A program is a means to reach a goal. It is like a road map showing you how to get from one place to another. You must design a specific program to reach your goals.

There are four principles to apply for success in developing a program to reach your goals.

Principle #1: Determining the goal

A thorough overview and discussion of all problems will help to identify the point at which to begin. From that first step, logical goals can be determined to solve the problems. Always begin with the simplest, easiest-to-attain goal first—in other words, build in success for yourself! You cannot work on many different goals at one time. For example, students may identify teen pregnancy, drag racing, and lack of drug-free activities as problems without recognizing that the easiest one to tackle at the beginning, and perhaps the underrlying problem, is the lack of drug-free activities.

Principle #2: List reasons for the goal

Listing reasons why the goal is important will in itself be a great motivator to help you achieve that goal. For example, drug-free activity is an important goal because it reduces boredom; offers safe, fun things to do; reduces use of harmful substances; and can save lives.

Principle #3: Describe goal in observable behavior

A goal must be clearly described; otherwise, there will be no way of knowing whether or not it was reached.

Example of an unclear goal: "We want to decrease the use of alcohol by students." This is vague, because it does not give you a way to measure the decrease or even to know if there indeed was a decrease.

Example of a clear goal: "Our goal is to make available to all students in our school chemical-free activities at least one weekend per month." This goal is clear—you will know if it is reached.

Principle #4: List steps to achieve the goal

In order to reach a goal, a number of steps have to be taken. These should be arranged so that the steps are listed in a logical order, from the simplest to the most difficult. For example, you have to make posters **before** you can hang them; you have to have all materials available **before** you can make the posters.

To take it a step further, look at this same program in even more detail. Let's say that the first chemical-free activity that the group decided on was a goofy, but fun, idea like having a Mad Hatter's Tea Party. The gimmick is that all students who come will have to wear their favorite hats, caps, scarves, or similar head coverings. Some people may show up in sombreros (large Mexican hats), ski caps, or bridal veils! It can be a hilarious party. Decorations should be inexpensive—posters designed on the Alice-in-Wonderland theme (it was in Wonderland that the Mad Hatter's Tea Party occurred), and balloons and hats hanging from the ceiling. Refreshments might be the usual soft drinks or mocktails (see appendix 1), plus hot spiced tea. And for entertainment: dancing, of course, and why not lessons by a student or guest for the Mexican Hat Dance?

The list of steps leading to a successful Mad Hatter's Tea Party may now look like this:
1. Mad Hatter's Tea Party
2. October 19 at 7:00 P.M.
3. Principal has given permission to use gym
4. Committees:
   Bob will supervise publicity (posters, announcements, etc.)
   Shayna will supervise selection and preparation of refreshments (hot spiced tea, dips and chips, cookies, soft drinks, etc.)
   Mike will supervise decorations (obtaining balloons and hats and hanging them from ceiling; mounting mural on wall, etc.)

WHEN TO SAY YES!

- Jesse is in charge of the entertainment (getting d.j. and records; inviting a guest or student to give the Mexican Hat Dance performance, etc.)
- Megan is responsible for financial activities (decisions on student admission charge, ticket sales; finding adult sponsors to contribute to costs of party; getting local business establishments to donate or pay for a d.j., food, and soft drinks)
- Jack will select and invite several teachers and parents to be present as sponsors, check about security, etc.

As you see, a lot is involved and much ongoing communication by and between committees is needed to reach the goal successfully.

An Example of Poor Guiding

Some of the graduating seniors at a certain high school decided to plan an all night chemical-free graduation. They immediately met with some resistance from classmates who said that no one would come if alcohol was not to be served. The seniors got discouraged as the plan fell apart. Their idea finally just faded away.

The problem here is obvious—there was no specific program to guide the students toward their goal. They also seemed fearful of standing up for what they felt was right. When you do not lay out plans on how you are going to reach a goal, any distraction can cause you to fail or to give up.

WHEN TO SAY YES!

An Example of Good Guiding

Read the article "The Kids Who Saved a Dying Town," by Bruce B. Henderson, in the September 1987 issue of *Reader's Digest* for an inspirational story about five sixth-graders who were given a class assignment to go on an "awareness walk" around their town of Royston, Georgia, and report on what they saw.

The report they gave their teacher, Alice Terry, was that six of the thirty-six buildings in the prime downtown area were vacant; there was litter everywhere; overgrown weeds and peeling paint was evident; and there were junked cars next to a city park. They thought their town was ugly and that somebody ought to do something about their dying town.

The teacher challenged the students to do something about this and reminded them that action, not talk, could solve the problem.

The students developed their program. They:
- wrote to public officials who might help;
- wrote to the owners of the vacant buildings, asking them to fix or sell their property or the students would report the buildings as fire hazards to the fire marshal;
- wrote railroad officials about the junked cars on land the railroad owned;
- asked the City Council to conduct a survey of town residents to find out what they wanted in their downtown area;
- made sketches to show what the buildings downtown would look like if restored;

- presented a skit to the fourth-, fifth-, and sixth-graders about the town history and asked them to help on a scheduled cleaning day.

The results of their project were impressive: the old buildings were sold, and the new owners restored them; junked cars were hauled off; new businesses started coming into the town; and 140 students and teachers showed up on cleaning day to sweep sidewalks, wash storefronts, pull up weeds, and plant flowers.

On September 26, 1986, these five students and their teacher received the Public Service Award of the U.S. Department of the Interior in Washington, D.C.

Youth can make a difference! These students guided their town in a positive direction by setting specific steps to reach their goal.

The third and last step in Phase III, Make Things Happen, is **networking. Networking** means gathering and uniting all available human resources in order to best reach your group goals. There is power and strength in numbers. If your school has an enrollment of a thousand students and only ten of you are working on making improvements there, progress will be very slow. But if you can get fifty or more students involved, you can make an impact. **Networking** is like having "connections"—knowing people, knowing whom to ask for support, knowing who can help Make Things Happen!

There are two guidelines for **networking.** One is that each group must have a goal for the group, and its members must have individual goals of their own. The other is that every member must make at least one "connection" with other individuals or organizations that can help the group reach its goals.

Who might the connections be? How should the connections be made? They may be made by sharing with friends information about your positive peer group, thereby getting them to join. It would help to get recognition for your group if the mayor of your city were to issue a proclamation about your group's achievements. Making connections might mean getting more teachers or counselors to support or sponsor your group, or getting parents to contribute time or money for your special projects. It might also mean by having some of your articulate members speak to groups such as the Lions Club, the Kiwanis, the Junior League, and the City Council to gather support for your group and its goals.

Once you communicate your group's goals to help your school, neighborhood, community, or, even, your country, you will be surprised at the willingness of other individuals and organizations to get behind you.

An Example of Poor Networking

Too many schools weaken their efforts by being divided, rather than united through **networking.**

A school may have, say, fifteen students who are trying to combat the problems of drinking and driving, with another group of, say, twenty promoting chemical-free activities, and still another group of, say, eighteen trying to educate classmates about the harmful effects of alcohol and other drugs.

If these three groups united through communicating and networking, there would be fifty-three students working together toward closely related goals. Using their combined energy, they would have a better chance of reaching their goals.

An Example of Good Networking

The SWAT (Students Working All Together) program began in September 1986 when I initially trained sixty students from Trinity and Bell high schools in the Hurst-Euless-Bedford Independent School District. For the initial membership, each club at the schools was asked to send two interested representatives to be a part of the SWAT teams. Later, others were selected at large from the student bodies. **Networking** was at its best as these SWAT members went back and shared with their clubs what they learned, and got more groups linked into the program. Six months later, an additional sixty students were trained. SWAT continues to grow, with hundreds on the contact list awaiting training. Recently, the group made a short video about SWAT to show to adult organizations when seeking their support.

A very successful project was produced by the Trinity High SWAT team. They called it DOA. Concerned about the drinking and driving that frequently occurs during the spring break (in Texas, especially, by youth who go to South Padre Island on the Gulf Coast), the SWAT team designed and put up posters in the school halls showing only the lower half of the bodies of what appeared to be a dead family (all you could see were legs: father in trousers, mother in skirt, kids in tennis shoes), and attached to one big toe of each body, a tag that read DOA (a term meaning "dead on arrival," used by hospitals on admission of someone deceased). These posters, though morbid, stimulated a lot of curiosity. Announcements over

WHEN TO SAY YES!

the public address system introduced the "family" and invited students to learn what happened to them during spring break. Students were invited for the next week to bring their lunches to the library, where a narrated slide show, developed by the SWAT group, showed the family packing for a trip, leaving, being hit by a car driven by a drinking teenager, being admitted to the hospital, and so forth. Several family members were listed in critical condition, but all survived in the end. The narrator said, "DOA can mean two things: dead on arrival or drive on alive. It's up to you." The audience was urged to not drink and to come back from spring break. Those who signed a commitment to do that received a key chain with "DOA" on it. Almost all the students did sign the commitment.

These students, by **networking**, are making a difference.

Now, in Phase III, you have learned the **goal setting, guiding,** and **networking** steps so that you can Make Things Happen. **Goal setting** gives you direction. **Guiding** helps you keep each other on track. Finally, **networking** gives you more strength to get to where you want to be.

MAKE THINGS HAPPEN

REMEMBER:

GOAL SETTING
GUIDING
NETWORKING

LEAD TO MAKING THINGS HAPPEN!

SUMMARY

SUMMARY

The How to Say No and Keep Your Friends program was designed to help you survive negative peer pressure. And by using it you are making wise choices for yourself and also serving as a role model to others. For many of you, however, that will not be enough. You will want more than just to survive; you will want to reach out and help others to survive.

WHEN TO SAY YES!

The When to Say Yes! program was designed for those of you—and there are a lot of you—who want more. You want to grow and you want to help others to grow. You truly understand that that is what living is about. You will go far in life because you are a "giver," not a "taker." Through your actions, you can help to make the ME generation into the WE generation.

There are many positive peer groups that I have helped to develop. Some of the names that they have selected for themselves tell their stories: SWAT (Students Working All Together), STOP (Student Thinking of Peers), H_2O (Help to Others), STARS (Students Teaching About the Risks of Smoking), TRY (Teen Relations and You), TAD (Teens Against Drugs), SWAPP (Students Working Against Peer Pressure), STAR (Students Taught About Awareness and Resistance), FUN (Friends-U-Need), and even the NURDS (Never Underestimate Really Determined Students)!

Never think that because you are young that you cannot make a difference. I continually hear about young people who are reaching out and helping. Just today I read in the paper about Jason Sutherland who died of leukemia at age fifteen. Nine of his classmates immediately went to work to raise money to help his parents with medical expenses. Through raffles, bake sales, and a dance, they raised $4,200 in three-and-a-half months. Before Jason died, he told his mother that if he could not live he wanted the money to go to research so other kids could live.

SUMMARY

That wish has been carried out: the money has been presented to Children's Medical City to be used for leukemia research.

This is a vivid example of reaching out. Jason, in his last wishes, reached out. Then his friends reached out to Jason's family and to others they will never know. Jason and his friends made a difference.

For good things like this to be accomplished the steps described in this book need to be followed. Those steps are:

CARING
PAIRING
SHARING
UNDERSTANDING
PRAISING
CONTRIBUTING
DEFINING PROBLEMS
GOAL SETTING
NETWORKING

SUMMARY

There will always be people in your life who will try to hold you back—a jealous sibling, an insecure friend, perhaps an alcoholic parent. They may not be intentionally holding you back—they may just not understand. It is your job to help yourself. You need to share and learn from those in your life who are constructive. It is your responsibility to create your own personal answers, while realizing that your decisions be constructive.

I am reminded of a letter I received in April, 1987, from a man who wrote me how people were trying to pressure him but he refused to let them stop him from doing good things. He asked for a free copy of my book, *Peer Pressure Reversal*. He wrote that he had no money but wanted the book to help him with volunteer work he did with delinquent boys. He signed his letter #313567; he was in prison.

He described the program, Operation Outreach, run by the chaplain, himself, and fourteen other inmates who work with delinquent boys "sentenced" by a judge to spend a day in prison. Through exposure to prison conditions and discussions, these men hope to convince others that they are on the road to destruction and help them change their lives.

I mailed the prisoner a book and told him that I wanted no money, only a report from him on how he used it. On May 5, 1987, I received his report. This is from the letter he mailed me:

Dear Mrs. Scott,

Greetings! I was glad to get your letter and book. I have started the book and will teach it and do a very good job of it. The boys we see need something like what you have to teach, because it is evident that many of them do not have proper guidance. I heard stories from some of these kids that would cause your hair to stand on end. Of course, many are exaggerating and, in some cases, out right lying. But, after being seven years in jail with some of the best liars, you learn to look at him, and if possible, speak to him and make a judgment on whether he could be possible trouble. I have become very good at this. I don't mean to sound arrogant. That isn't it at all. In here it's called SURVIVAL.

I would like to tell you little about myself, so that you will have a general idea of where I am headed. I'm 30 years-old and have been here for seven years. I have a 25 year sentence that I should be paroled on within the next 18–20 months. I have taken college classes here in prison and am fifteen hours away from my associate degree. I plan to major in psychology and sociology and want to become a youth counselor in a church someday. I have tried to utilize my time as well as possible.

We also have peer pressure in here and I can't begin to tell you how the others tease you because you are going to school and trying to help yourself and help others. I have been called everything from "school boy" to names that I won't mention. So I have had to use peer pressure reversal methods and until your book never really realized I was doing it. I have hung tough though and am going to make it. The world is there for those who want to grab it. You just have to want to grab it. We, as Americans, tend to take things for granted and just not have the drive we should.

Thank you for your concern and please feel free to offer suggestions that might help me. I take a great deal of pride in what I do. God bless you and please try to visit our program sometime.

Sincerely,
#313567

Look who is trying to hold this man back—other inmates! They should be congratulating him on concentrating on his education, trying to make something of himself, and trying to reach out into the community and help others from making his mistakes. Why don't they congratulate him? Jealousy? Fear of failure? "Macho" attitude? Fear of being teased? Probably all of these reasons. And all of these reasons are **poor** reasons. They defeat the other prisoners and, if #313567 let them, they could defeat him and his efforts. But he is handling it and I think he will make it. He added that the program was an inspiration for him and helped him toward his own personal rehabilitation. He had goals and dreams he never had before and offers from judges and probation officers to help find the right job when he was released.

WHEN TO SAY YES!

Look and you will see all nine steps of the When to Say Yes! program in his efforts.

You are of course free to grow, but you must understand the implications of freedom. You must move in a positive, constructive direction with your decisions. Society will not allow destructive people the freedom to destroy. In other words, you are becoming responsible. You will be held accountable for the decisions that you make. But as long as you know the difference between good and bad, right and wrong, then you are capable of setting positive goals and making things happen. You are helping the world around you grow in ways that are important to you. Life will be exciting in a brand new way. What a reason for living!

APPENDIXES

Appendix 1

RECIPES FOR "MOCKTAILS"
(NONALCOHOLIC DRINKS)

Golden Glow Punch
- 1   3-ounce package orange-flavored gelatin
- 4   cups water
- 1   6-ounce package frozen pineapple-orange juice concentrate
- 4   cups apple juice
- 1   1-pint 12-ounce bottle (3½ cups) ginger ale, chilled

Dissolve gelatin in 1 cup boiling water. Stir in pineapple-orange concentrate. Add apple juice and 3 cups cold water. Carefully pour in chilled ginger ale. Makes about twenty-five 4-ounce servings.

Quick Punch
- 1   quart sherbet (any fruit flavor)
- 3   1-pint 12-ounce bottle lemon-lime carbonated beverage

Scoop sherbet into a punch bowl. Carefully add the carbonated beverage. Ladle into punch cups. Makes 25 to 30 four-ounce servings.

Tallahassee Tonic
- 1⅓ cup orange juice
- 1½ cup tonic water
- Ice
- Orange or lime wedge

Pour orange juice and tonic water over ice in tall glass. Garnish with orange wedge, if desired. Serves 2.

Orange Macaroon Delight
- 2 cups orange juice
- 2 cups crushed ice
- ½ cup canned coconut cream
- ¾ teaspoon almond extract
- Sweetened whipped cream
- Orange peel, shredded

In blender, combine orange juice, ice, coconut cream, and almond extract. Cover and blend. Serve in chilled glasses. Garnish with whipped cream and shredded orange peel, if desired. Serves 4.

Merry Berry Holiday Punch
- 6 cups orange juice
- 2 cups cranberry juice cocktail
- 2 10-ounce packages frozen strawberries in syrup
- 3 cups ginger ale
- Ice
- Orange slices, fresh strawberries and mint (optional)

In large bowl, combine orange juice, cranberry juice, and strawberries. Add ginger ale and ice just before serving. If desired, float orange slices, strawberries, and mint on top. Serves about 18.

Appendix 2

Hi!

I am interested in who you are and what skills you used from my book. Please answer the following questions, and mail your answers to my office: 5521 Hidalgo Court, Garland, Texas 75043.

1. What did you like best about When to Say Yes!?

2. Which skills did you start using and how did they help you?

3. Did you make a new friend, join a group, or start a positive peer group? If so, tell me about it.

4. Are you a part of a positive peer group at your school? What is its name? What does the group do to help others?

Thank you!

> Best wishes,
> Sharon Scott, L.P.C., President
> Sharon Scott and Associates

Appendix 3

Services for Groups

Sharon Scott is available in any of the following capacities:

- Keynote speaker
- Workshop leader
- Consultant on developing positive peer groups

If you are interested in having her speak to your group or to purchase her video, write for information to:

Sharon Scott and Associates
5521 Hidalgo Court
Garland, TX 75043

Appendix 4

Books Available

Sharon Scott has written the following books:

- How to Say No and Keep Your Friends
- Peer Pressure Reversal
- Positive Peer Groups

For price information or to order any of these titles, call or write:

Human Resource Development Press
22 Amherst Road
Amherst, MA 01002
1-800-822-2801 (outside Massachusetts)
(413) 253-3488 (within Massachusetts)

Discounts given on quantity orders.